Ron & Atie van der Meer

OH LORD!

CROWN PUBLISHERS, INC. | NEW YORK

Published in the United States in 1980. Copyright © 1979 by The Felix Gluck
Press Ltd. Twickenham. Published in Great Britain in 1979. All rights reserved.
No part of this publication may be reproduced, stored in a retrieval system, or
transmitted, in any form or by any means, electronic, mechanical, photocopying,
recording, or otherwise, without prior written permission of the publisher. In-
quiries should be addressed to Crown Publishers, Inc., One Park Avenue, New
York, N.Y. 10016. Manufactured in the United States of America. Published
simultaneously in Canada by General Publishing Company Limited.

10 9 8 7 6 5 4 3 2 1

Library of Congress Cataloging in Publication Data
Van der Meer, Ron, 1945-   Oh Lord!   Summary: Relates the daily activi-
ties of God and two small and lively angels while He creates the world.
[1. Creation—Fiction] I. Van der Meer, Atie, joint author. II. Title.
PZ7.V28390h   1980   [E]   79-24493   ISBN 0-517-54006-1.

OH LORD!

In the beginning the Lord God was asleep and dreaming happily.

Suddenly two of His smallest angels woke Him up. This was a very important day.

"Stop it!"

"I warn you!"

"Right, that will teach you a lesson."

But the Lord felt better after a shower and a good breakfast.

He was ready to begin creating Heaven and Earth.   First He made a few drawings...

and then a few more,

until at last He was

satisfied.

"I've got it!" He cried. "Let's start ."

Outside, He started to draw the earth, but it was too dark to see properly.

So He made light, and separated the day from the night.

Next day He drew the universe and the clouds in the sky.

On the third day He put dry land in the seas and . . .

created all the plants and trees that grow on earth.

On the fourth day He made the sun to shine in the day and the moon and stars at night.

On the fifth day He created all the birds that fly in the air and all the creatures swimming in the seas.

Then they stood back to admire their work. It was much more fun now.

On the sixth day the Lord took a clean apron and a large lump of clay.
"Today I must model some land animals," He told the angels.

"Land animals?"

"I know."

"No I don't!"

"Oh Lord!"

"What on earth are they?"

"Wait, I must think!"

"I must think very hard."

"That's it. I've got it!"

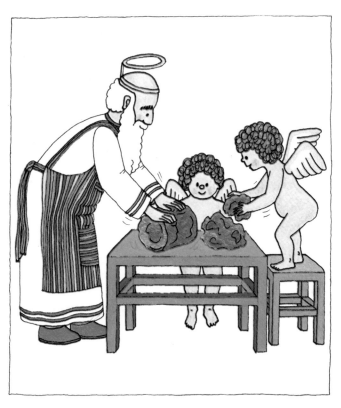

"Now you roll that into a ball,

while I put a bit here and a bit there."

"Don't you like it?"   "Oh Lord, something's missing!"

"Look, Lord, we've finished it for you."   "Beautiful. That's exactly the cat I had in mind."

"Come on, let's go and paint it."

"I think I'll make it a ginger cat."

"It looks nice. Can we play with it?"

"Yes, but first I have to breathe life into it."

"Good Heavens!"

Soon the next land animal was ready to be painted.

The angels were proud of their artistic effort, but the Lord was not at all pleased.

He told them to repaint it at once.

They had just done that,

when the Lord produced His next animal.

The angels made a good start, but a little accident finished it for them. All it needed was a

bit of yellow here,

a bit of pink there.

"That's perfect!" said the Lord. "Let's make some more."

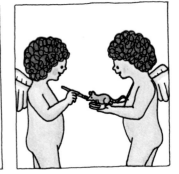

So they did.   Lots more.   Some big, some small, some tiny

and some ENORMOUS.

Unfortunately, not every animal was a complete success.

The Lord breathed life into it . . .   then wished He hadn't.

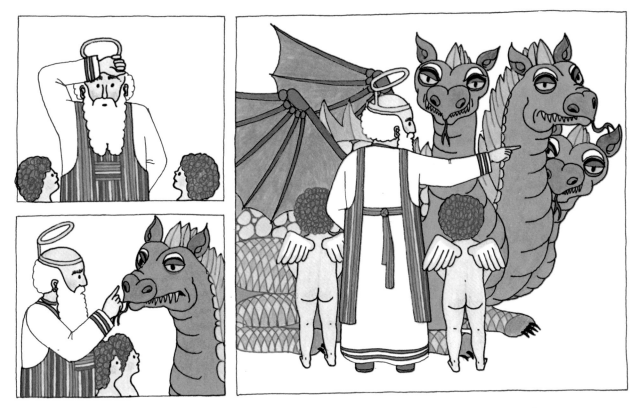

He was so furious that He told it to go away and join all the other rejects.

But one of the angels thought it was a pity some of these animals couldn't live on earth.

"Now for something special."   But what?"

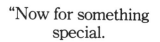

"I know . . .   something like me!"

"Look out!" said the Lord.

"Help!"

"This animal seems like me?" said the Lord.

"But such a nose and those ears . . ."

"What a gorilla!

I look much better."

So the Lord tried again, using one of His angels as a model.

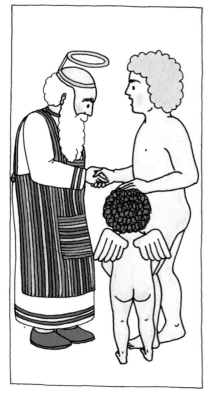

"I'll call you Adam," He said.

Adam didn't much like
the gorilla.

"Sorry. I'll make you a
better partner."

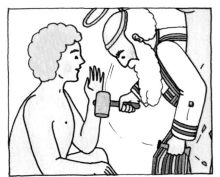

Adam got more and more excited.

"You can model for me now."

He thought it was a masterpiece.

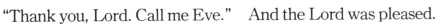

"I've done it!" He said.

"Thank you, Lord. Call me Eve."   And the Lord was pleased.   "Let's go . . .

to the Garden of Eden."

Then . . .

on the seventh day the Lord had a well-earned rest.